Whimsical Accents for Your Home

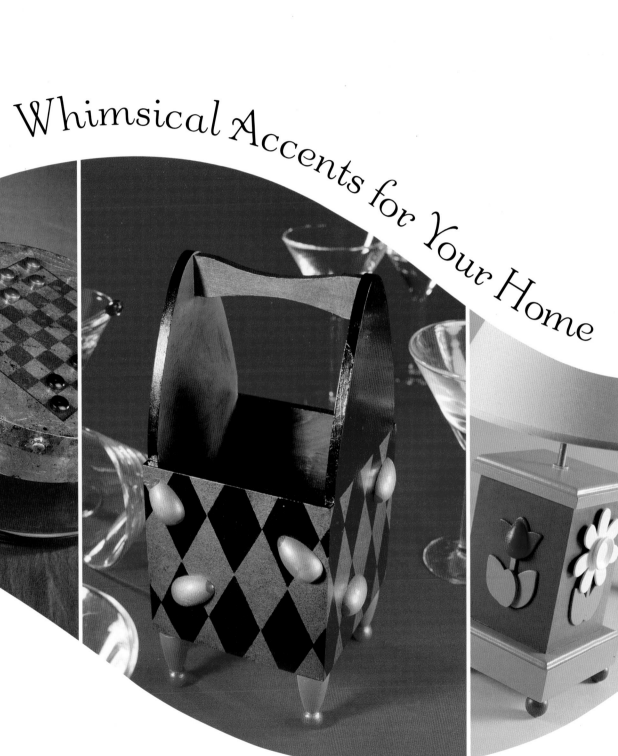

 NORTH LIGHT BOOKS
CINCINNATI, OHIO
www.artistsnetwork.com

JEFF McWILLIAMS

ABOUT THE AUTHOR

Jeff McWilliams is well known for his dramatic studio set designs, trade show booths and furniture creations. Jeff has created two successful furniture lines, featured in the books of Donna Dewberry, the "Sweet Dreams Bedroom Collection" and the "Furniture Fantasy Collection." His private collections, "Dry Grass," "Dragonfly" and "Birdhouse," have been featured in *Better Homes and Gardens* and on the Lynette Jennings show. He is currently working on the "Kid's Kingdom Collection." Jeff works out of a design studio in Norcross, Georgia, and has authored several books on furniture and painted accessories. For more information, visit Jeff's website: www.jmdonline.net.

08 07 06 05 04   5 4 3 2 1

Library of Congress Cataloging-in-Publication Data

McWilliams, Jeff.
    Whimsical accents for your home /Jeff McWilliams.
            p. cm.
    Includes index.
    ISBN 1-58180-590-X (alk. paper)
        1. Acrylic painting–Technique. 2. Decoration and ornament.
3. Painted woodwork. 4. House furnishings. I. Title.

TT385.M385 2004
745.593--dc22   2004043364

EDITOR: Tonia Davenport
COVER DESIGNER: Marissa Bowers
INTERIOR DESIGNER: Brian Roeth
LAYOUT ARTIST: Kathy Gardner
PRODUCTION COORDINATOR: Sara Dumford
PHOTOGRAPHER: Tim Grondin
STYLIST: Nora Martini

METRIC CONVERSION CHART

to convert	to	multiply by
Inches	Centimeters	2.54
Centimeters	Inches	0.4
Feet	Centimeters	30.5
Centimeters	Feet	0.03
Yards	Meters	0.9
Meters	Yards	1.1
Sq. Inches	Sq. Centimeters	6.45
Sq. Centimeters	Sq. Inches	0.16
Sq. Feet	Sq. Meters	0.09
Sq. Meters	Sq. Feet	10.8
Sq. Yards	Sq. Meters	0.8
Sq. Meters	Sq. Yards	1.2
Pounds	Kilograms	0.45
Kilograms	Pounds	2.2
Ounces	Grams	28.4
Grams	Ounces	0.035

This book is dedicated to my parents, Thomas and Jackie McWilliams. In all my many years, and in all of the directions my life has taken, they have supported me. I have had the opportunity to achieve many things and encounter many places because of their loving encouragement. I can never return the kindness and sacrifices that have been made on my behalf throughout my lifetime. For that I am grateful. Thank you, I love you both very much, Jeff.

DEDICATION

ACKNOWLEDGMENTS

I would like to take the opportunity to acknowledge all those who assisted in the production of this book. Thanks to the following:

Tricia Waddell at North Light Books, for your hard work and understanding throughout this project and others we have worked on together. Patrick, thanks for allowing me to run things by you to make sure I was on track, and for letting me know when I had "missed." Thomas and Dad, thanks for the assembly of all the parts. What a process to put the pieces together and help with all the knobs and feet! My family: Jackie, Thomas, Chris, Andrew, Heather and Asher, thanks for supporting me in all of my endeavors throughout my life and for providing me with encouragement along the way. My grandparents Thomas and Alice Poole, and my Texas mama Jean, thanks for always being there for me. Jane Gauss, thanks for being one of the kindest people I know.

Thanks also to my friends at Plaid Enterprises who have provided support and materials for this book, and to Chris at Walnut Hollow, Doris at Wayne's Woodenware, Provo Craft, Bear With Us, Water Color Walls and Lara's Crafts for all the wooden pieces.

TABLE OF CONTENTS

INTRODUCTION

The projects in this book represent a variety of great designs and finishes for creating amazing furniture and accessories for yourself or others. Each project is easy to do and offers a perfect opportunity for beginners to get a taste of painted home décor. Working together on one of these projects could also make a great family activity.

The projects range in complexity and employ multiple finishes including color washing, silver leafing, stamping, stencilling and a variety of faux finishes. Using paint and a variety of tools, you can give new life to old items or create fantastic new works of art that you and your family can enjoy for years to come.

Follow the step-by-step instructions to accomplish these great new ideas, and don't be afraid to put your own spin on things. Have fun being your own designer. Follow existing color schemes from your home or from a special item in a room to develop dynamic color palettes for your projects. Use the ideas in this book to create gifts for that special friend or for an entire family.

I have always welcomed the opportunity to create, inspired by colors and different artisitic concepts. These projects are natural extensions of the creative energy bursting within me. I hope you enjoy this book as much as I have enjoyed sharing my bursts of inspiration with you.

There is a lot more to painting than paint alone. Brushes and various mediums will have as much of an impact on your projects as the colors will. On these pages are listed the basic materials you will want to have ready before beginning the projects. All of the items will be available from either your local art and craft supply store or hardware store.

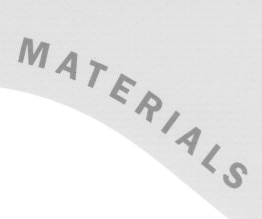

Paints

Acrylic paint is easy to use and comes in convenient plastic squeeze bottles. Its creamy, smooth texture and great coverage make it a good choice for quickly painted projects. Acrylics are perfect for mixing and provide easy cleanup with soap and water. They can be found at any craft or art store or can be purchased online.

Use the suggested colors to guide you or try other color combinations based on your own creative style and house décor.

For all the projects in this book I used either Plaid FolkArt or Apple Barrel acrylic paints. Plaid has a great color palette across paint lines so finding a color of choice is never a problem. When working with larger pieces that require more than just a few ounces of paint, I just take my favorite color to the paint store and have a can mixed to match.

Mediums

Several acrylic-based mediums will be used for the projects in this book. While paint is the foundation for the color of a project, other mediums such as these add interest and texture, as well as protection.

Découpage Medium

Use this to cover wooden surfaces with pieces of decorative paper and to provide a protective finish. It's also good for sealing a surface before applying antiquing medium, which I'll discuss next.

My medium of choice for découpage projects is Mod Podge by Plaid. I'm convinced there was Mod Podge on the Mayflower with the Pilgrims and on the ark with the animals! I used it for several projects in this book.

Antiquing Medium

This is a type of stain that settles into cracks on a surface to give it an aged look. It is brushed on and then wiped off, leaving a subtle brownish cast on parts of the surface. I used Plaid's Down Home Brown for several projects in this book.

Crackle Medium

One of my favorite finishes comes from this medium, because it makes anything more interesting, whether it produces a subtle texture or dramatic cracks. It is used widely throughout this book. The secret for successful crackling is to use several very thick coats. Never let the finish drip (you will have to pay attention to achieve an even coat) and don't let the medium dry too long. There are several types of crackle medium on the market, but I have had the best results with the Plaid brand. Years ago I was scared of this finish and avoided it at all costs, but after using Plaid FolkArt Crackle Medium, I now add crackle to any project I can.

Acrylic Varnish

This medium preserves your work. You can choose from a variety of finishes, depending on whether you want your piece to look glossy or just plain finished. I feel a piece is not complete until the varnish pulls everything together with a balanced sheen. There are many brush-on varnishes available that work well for sealing and protecting surfaces, in addition to the spray variety. I like to use FolkArt Matte or Gloss Spray Acrylic for smooth, even coverage.

Brushes

Brushes come in a wide variety of sizes, but the ones I use the most often are the 2-inch (51mm) flat, the 1-inch (25mm) flat, the $^3/_4$-inch (19mm) flat and the $^1/_2$-inch (12mm) flat. All the brushes you will ever need can be found at your local craft or art store. I use a no. 1 liner brush for details and lettering. I have chosen to use Plaid One Stroke Brushes, which are good quality, durable brushes that are not too expensive.

Stencil brushes are round and have very short bristles. They come in different sizes just like the flat brushes. Most of the stencils used for the projects in this book require a $^1/_2$-inch (12mm) stencil brush, but if you choose to use a larger stencil that requires a lot of paint, you may want to use a larger stencil brush.

Stencils

There are lots of stencil patterns on the market. It seems to me that most stencils are of equal quality, so it is fine to just pick patterns you like. I used several multiple-layer stencils as well as some single layers for background texture in these projects. Use stencil tape to mask off any parts of the stencil that will not be used when painting. Stencils are available at craft and art supply stores. Home improvement stores also carry a variety of stencils.

General Supplies

In addition to paint and brushes, there are a few additional materials you will want to have on hand. These materials are every bit as important as the previously mentioned supplies.

Sponges

I used natural sea sponges for several projects in this book, for finishing and for antiquing larger surfaces. Sponges can also provide an interesting texture when used to apply paint.

Sandpaper

I use medium-grade sandpaper for preparing surfaces and sanding between coats. A sanding block offers easy sanding around corners and on larger surfaces.

Wood Glue

Wood glue is used to adhere wooden glue-ons to your projects and to assemble furniture or other pieces with multiple parts. It is water soluble and bonds wood to wood with a very strong hold.

Painters' Tape

Painters' tape is used for masking off areas as well as for making strip templates. I have used several different widths, but found $^1/_2$" (12mm) and 1" (25mm) to work well for most projects.

Before beginning any of the projects in this book, you should have an understanding of the basic techniques used throughout them. Preparing a wood surface by filling, sanding and sealing is the most important part of any project to ensure a finished piece of good quality. After the prep work is done, the fun begins! The techniques that will be used to create each project are explained below. Combining one or more of these treatments is fun to do and really makes for a striking effect.

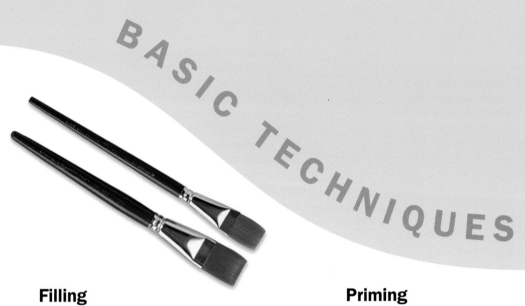

BASIC TECHNIQUES

Filling

Visible holes or nicks in the surface of a piece can be diminished using wood filler. This is the first step for preparing your wooden surface. Use a small palette knife or your finger to spread wood filler into the damaged area, then wait for the filler to dry and sand it smooth. If the area appears sunken after drying, add a second coat and let it dry before sanding.

Sanding

Before applying any paint or medium to a raw wood surface, the wood should be sanded using a medium-grade sandpaper. Smoothing out naturally occurring splinters and other minor flaws will give your piece a nice surface to paint on. This will not only protect your surface from having a splinter pulled off (thus damaging your newly painted surface) but will protect your hands from future splinters as well. Use a tack cloth or dry towel to remove the dust from the surface before applying any paint.

Gluing

Wood glue will bond wood to wood whether your project is painted or unpainted. Before applying any glue, be sure the surface is as clean as possible. Excess sawdust can be wiped away with a damp cloth. Let the glue dry completely before you proceed to do any painting. Wet glue is easily cleaned up with water.

Priming

Acrylic-based gesso may be used to give an opaque finish when the surface of the project is not a light shade to begin with and several coats of paint will be required to create pure bright color. Priming also prevents the wood from acting like a sponge and absorbing the first layer of paint.

Basecoating

Apply a basecoat by brushing paint in the direction of the grain of the wood. Let it dry completely. Sand the surface with medium-grade sandpaper again, sanding with the grain of the wood. Use a tack cloth or dry towel to remove the dust from the surface before applying the next coat of paint. Sanding between the first and second basecoats controls the raised wood grain, allowing a smoother painted surface.

Découpaging

This involves applying fabric or paper to a surface and then covering the surface with a finish. This process can be used to create background texture color and design to various projects. You can use découpage to add bits and pieces of different images to a project or to completely cover an entire surface. In the past, découpage was created with glue and many layers of varnish, but today great results can be achieved with specialized products and fewer steps.

Distressing and Crackling

A distressed surface adds character and an aged look to a new piece of furniture or wooden object. You can create a simple distressed finish by painting a piece with several different layers of color, then sanding or scraping the piece after the paint has dried to allow several undercoats to be seen. Finally, sand the edges where natural wear would occur. This allows the wood surface itself to show through the layers of paint. Do not basecoat with primer if you are planning to distress the finish. The process of distressing works well for projects that might not have the best surface to begin with: You can use the flaws in the piece as a plus.

The natural process of crackling comes from years of exposure to wind and weather, but the effect can be created in a few minutes with crackle medium. The age and character of this rustic finish can be created easily on any solid surface. The simplest way to add this unique texture is to apply one layer of crackle medium over the basecoat. Then add varnish, and antique the surface once the crackle medium and the varnish have dried. Another method is to use two layers of crackle medium over the basecoat, adding a coat of contrasting paint over all. The topcoat of paint will shrink as it dries, forming an uneven, crackled finish. This application works as well for dramatic contemporary pieces as it does for traditional, country-style pieces.

Weathered, yet sophisticated, this birdhouse provides eye-catching charm with the use of crackle medium.

Metallic Leafing

This is a great way to add a metallic finish to a variety of painted and unpainted surfaces. Use metallic leafing sheets and the manufacturer's suggested adhesive for dramatic results. Leafing supplies can be found at most art and craft stores.

Staining and Antiquing

Staining adds color and warmth to wood surfaces while allowing the natural wood grain to show through. You may stain an entire surface, or apply it randomly as an accent. Using a rag or foam brush, apply stain liberally and then wipe off the excess with a clean rag. The porosity of the wood and the length of time the stain is allowed to soak into the wood will determine the depth of color in the finish.

Antiquing a piece is done in the same way and the medium can be applied over a painted surface after the paint is completely dry, adding dimension to the finish of the project. The antiquing medium can be left on the surface to remain as dark or as light as you choose to make it. Always test stains and antiquing mediums on a practice surface before applying color to your project; it is always easier to add more color than to remove it after the finish has dried.

Stamping

A quick and easy way to add personality to a painted surface is to use rubber or foam stamps to create exciting images. The variety of stamps on the market makes it easy to mix and match different patterns together for a unique result. It is a good idea to stamp the design on a piece of paper before stamping your project. Acrylic craft paint works well for stamping when applied to the stamp sparingly.

Stencilling

Stencilling is another great way to add design to a painted surface. Using a low-tack stencil tape, secure the stencil to the surface where you wish to add the image. Use a circular or pouncing motion to apply paint with a stencil brush, through the holes of the stencil. Pounce off excess paint onto a paper towel before applying the brush to the project's surface. Use more pressure to create darker areas in the stencil image.

Finishing

Applying a protective sealer to your completed project will ensure easy care and cleaning. Use several thin coats rather than one heavy coat. Whether you choose a brush-on varnish or a spray sealer, be sure to use it in a well-ventilated area, and protect all underlying surfaces from splashes or overspray.

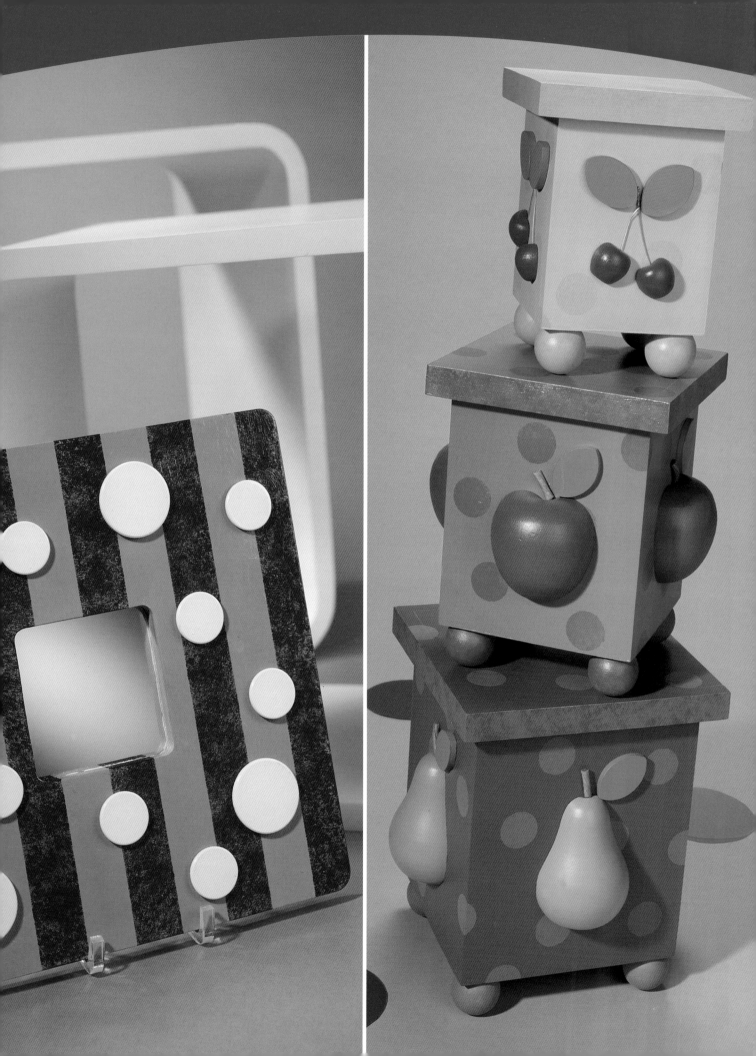

Color Explosion

When it comes to color, sometimes nothing is more gratifying than to drown ourselves in it. Brightly colored accents around our home tell the world that we are creative, bold and unafraid to express ourselves. A whimsically-styled piece can also serve as a reminder to not take ourselves too seriously.

The projects in this section are all easy to complete, and will encourage you to dive into the world of painted home décor. Whether you make these for yourself or as gifts, you won't be able to avoid having fun becoming immersed in bright hues and maybe even a little silliness while completing these projects. Go ahead and unleash your secret love of intense color! Go play!

Funky Floral Lamp

This lamp with its whimsical floral decorations can brighten a bedroom or study. Turn the lamp around each quarter for a new flower design.

Materials

lamp base
(Wayne's Woodenware)

light kit

wooden glue-ons:
    1 posy (Provo Crafts)
    1 round cap (Lara's Crafts)
    7 micro mini apples (Lara's Crafts)
    3 tulips (Provo Crafts)
    1 daisy (Provo Crafts)
    1 plate (Lara's Crafts)
    1 flower (Provo Crafts)
    1 doll head, 1" (25mm) (Lara's Crafts)
    1 split pigeon egg (Lara's Crafts)
    1 egg oval, small (Lara's Crafts)

FolkArt Paints:
    Dark Hydrangea
    Hydrangea
    Lipstick Red
    Winter White

FolkArt Artists' Pigments:
    Yellow Citron

$\frac{1}{2}$-inch (12mm) flat brush

1-inch (25mm) flat brush

medium-grade sandpaper

tack cloth

wood glue

matte spray sealer

1. Sand and prep the lamp surface. Using the 1-inch (25mm) flat brush, paint the center section of the lamp base with Dark Hydrangea. Apply two coats, sanding lightly between coats.

2. Paint the bottom and top sections of the lamp base with Yellow Citron. Paint the feet with Lipstick Red.

3. Using the $\frac{1}{2}$-inch (12mm) flat brush, paint the posy leaves and stem with Yellow Citron and the ball top with Hydrangea. Paint both the round cap and all of the apples with Lipstick Red.

4. Paint the three tulip stems and leaves with Yellow Citron. Paint the tops of one of the tulips with Lipstick Red. Leave the other two unpainted (their flower portions will be covered up with other glue-ons in step 7).

5. Paint the daisy and the plate with Winter White. When the paint is dry, glue the plate to the center of the daisy.

6. Paint the flower and the 1" (25mm) doll head with Hydrangea. When dry, glue the doll head to the center of the flower. Paint the split pigeon egg with Lipstick Red, and glue to the center of the red-painted tulip, when dry. Paint the small oval egg with Yellow Citron, and glue it to the center of the red tulip's leaves, when dry.

7. Glue the daisy and flower over the two unpainted tulip heads. Glue one complete flower to each of the four sides of the lamp. Glue the mini apples around the outside of the posy head.

8. Spray the lamp with sealer for protection. After the lamp dries, add the light kit, following the directions on the package.

Tip

"Baby wipe" products that contain alcohol are great for removing paint from your hands, brush handles, and sometimes even a slight mistake from a project. Plaid has developed a special "wipe" product made just for painters.

Fruit "Punch" Boxes

Brighten up any room with these wonderful fruit boxes. The fruit comes to life and practically jumps from the sides of the boxes. A subtle tone-on-tone pattern underneath complements the effect.

Materials

wooden stacking boxes
(Wayne's Woodenware)

wooden glue-ons:
 12 ball feet, ³⁄₄" (19mm)
 16 footballs (Lara's Crafts)
 8 cherries (Bear With Us)
 4 apple halves (Bear With Us)
 4 pear halves (Bear With Us)

FolkArt Paints:
 Azure Blue
 Cayman Blue
 Green
 Lipstick Red
 Peony
 Poppy Red
 School Bus Yellow

FolkArt Artists' Pigments:
 Butler Magenta
 Yellow Citron
 Yellow Light

natural fiber handle from a paper
shopping bag

¹⁄₂-inch (12mm) flat brush

¹⁄₂-inch (12mm) stencil brush

1-inch (25mm) flat brush

medium-grade sandpaper

matte spray sealer

floral cutters

circle stencil, 1" (25mm)

stencil tape

tack cloth

wood glue

craft wire

CHERRIES BOX

1. Sand and prep the small box. Using the 1-inch (25mm) flat brush, paint the entire surface of the box and four of the ³⁄₄" (19mm) ball feet with two coats of Yellow Light. Paint the inside of the box as well; you never know when someone may look inside. Sand lightly between the first and second coats for a smooth finish.

2. Using the circle stencil and the ¹⁄₂-inch (12mm) stencil brush, pounce School Bus Yellow onto the sides and the top of the box. Cover the box randomly with no specific quantity of circles. Randomly pounce School Bus Yellow onto the edge of the box top and on the four ball feet. This will give a textured finish.

3. Using the ¹⁄₂-inch (12mm) flat brush, paint eight of the footballs with Green and eight cherries with Lipstick Red. Use two coats for best coverage.

4. Cut four 5" (13cm) lengths of craft wire. Fold each in half, twisting about ³⁄₄" (19mm) together at the fold to create the thick top portion of the stem.

5. Once all the paint is dry, glue on the cherries, leaves and stems. Be careful not to use too much glue to avoid having it show.

6. Glue one ball foot to each of the four bottom corners of the box.

7. Spray with matte spray sealer for protection.

APPLE AND PEAR BOXES

1. For the Apple Box, begin with the medium box, and follow steps 1 and 2 from Cherries Box, substituting Cayman Blue for the surface of the box, and Azure Blue for the stencilling and ball feet. For the Pear Box, begin with the large box, and substitute Peony for the surface of the box and Butler Magenta for the stencilling and ball feet.

2. Paint the four apple halves with Poppy Red and the four pear halves with Yellow Citron. Paint eight footballs with Green. Two coats of paint provide best coverage.

3. Cut four 1" (25mm) sections of the handle from the paper shopping bag for the apple and pear stems. The more the handle curves the better.

4. Attach the apple and pear halves, leaves and stems to the sides of their own boxes with wood glue. Glue the matching ball feet on the bottom corners of each box.

5. Spray the boxes with matte spray sealer for protection.

Tiny Bubbles Mirror

Think "retro fun" with this bubble-inspired mirror. This would be a catchy wall treatment in a bright bathroom or at counter level in a kitchen.

Materials

wooden square frame
(Walnut Hollow)

wooden glue-ons:
  5 circles, 1" (25mm)
  (Lara's Crafts)
  7 circles, 1³/₄" (44mm)
  (Lara's Crafts)

mirror, cut to size of frame opening

FolkArt Paints:
  Coastal Blue
  Winter White

FolkArt Artists' Pigments:
  Brilliant Ultramarine

¹/₂-inch (12mm) stencil brush

1-inch (25mm) flat brush

painters' tape

medium-grade sandpaper

tack cloth

wood glue

matte spray sealer

high-gloss spray sealer

1. Sand and prep the frame. Using the 1-inch (25mm) flat brush, paint two coats of Coastal Blue on the surface of the frame, sanding lightly between coats.

2. Place strips of painters' tape vertically across the surface of the frame, lining up the edges of each strip side to side. Now remove every other piece of tape. This will be the quickest you have ever made perfectly spaced lines. With the stencil brush, pounce Brilliant Ultramarine onto the spaces between the strips, but do not cover the undercoat solidly. This creates a textured effect. When the paint is dry, remove the strips of tape and spray the surface with matte spray sealer.

3. Paint the circles with two coats of Winter White, sanding between coats. When the paint is completely dry, spray the circles with high-gloss spray sealer. This will provide a more contemporary finish for the project.

4. Attach the circles to the surface of the frame with wood glue. Add the mirror to the frame and you have a bold funky mirror. You can find small sections of mirror at a hardware store or local glass company.

Tip

Waiting for varnish to dry is especially hard on those of us who crave instant gratification. Even though you may be anxious, resist the urge to use a hair dryer to speed the drying process. When exposed to heat, varnish has a tendency to crack, so it's really best to wait.

Field of Daisies Clock

Keep the look of fresh flowers in the room all year round with this clock overflowing with tiny white daisies. It won't be hard keeping up with the time with this great piece.

Materials

wooden clock surface
("Carriage Clock," Walnut Hollow)

clock parts (Walnut Hollow)

wooden glue-ons:
23 micro daisies (Lara's Crafts)
3 lighthouses (Lara's Crafts)
1 round cap, 1½" (38mm)
1 ball, 1¼" (32mm)

Apple Barrel Paints:
Apricot

FolkArt Paints:
Fresh Foliage
Lemon Custard
Winter White

½-inch (12mm) flat brush

1-inch (25mm) flat brush

medium-grade sandpaper

tack cloth

wood glue

matte spray sealer

1. Sand and prep the clock surface. Basecoat the entire clock surface with Winter White. Sand and add a second coat for best results.

2. Paint the top and bottom of the clock body with Apricot.

3. Paint Lemon Custard around the center of the clock.

4. Remove the square center from the clock's housing, and using the 1-inch (25mm) flat brush, paint it with two coats of Fresh Foliage, sanding lightly between coats. When it is dry, replace it in the clock's housing.

5. Paint the micro daisies with two coats of Winter White. Dot the centers with Lemon Custard, using the handle end of a large paintbrush.

6. For the feet, paint the body of the lighthouses with Fresh Foliage and the detail ring with Lemon Custard. Paint the top cap with Apricot.

7. Paint the round cap with Fresh Foliage and the ball with Lemon Custard.

8. Arrange the flowers over the entire square center of the clock, then glue them in place. Glue the lighthouses, top cap down, onto the bottom of the clock. Glue the ball and the round cap to the top of the clock. Refer to the photo for specific placement.

9. Spray the clock with matte spray sealer for protection.

10. Attach the clock parts following the directions on the package. You will need a battery to make the clock run.

Tip

For projects that have removable inserts, such as this piece, or any ready-made frame, having the temporary, flexible points either break or fall out can be frustrating. A staple gun works great to refit items into their original housing. Be sure to hold the gun about ½" (12mm) away from the surface when shooting, or the staple will go all the way in.

Chicken Coop Cabinet

Thoughts of the farm, bold and bright, are captured in this chicken-inspired cupboard. This cabinet could be used to brighten up the walls in the kitchen.

Materials

wooden cabinet with chicken wire door (Provo Crafts)

wooden glue-ons:
    1 rooster with a metal wing (Provo Crafts)
    11 robin egg halves (Lara's Crafts)

FolkArt Paints:
    Lipstick Red
    School Bus Yellow
    Wicker White

FolkArt Artists' Pigments:
    Pure Black

no. 1 liner brush

½-inch (12mm) flat brush

1-inch (25mm) flat brush

painters' tape

medium-grade sandpaper

tack cloth

wood glue

matte spray sealer

1. Remove the door from the cabinet. Sand and prep both, then using Pure Black, basecoat the sides, front and back of the cabinet, inside and out. Sand lightly, and then paint on a second coat of Pure Black.

2. Paint the shelves and top of the cabinet with Lipstick Red, applying two coats. Sand lightly between coats.

3. Paint the frame of the door with School Bus Yellow. It might be easier to use painters' tape to protect the wire as you paint around the inside edges. You don't want to get paint on the wire because it does not come off easily.

4. Paint the body and head of the rooster with Pure Black and the comb with Lipstick Red. Use Wicker White and the handle end of the ½-inch (12mm) paintbrush for the dots on the rooster's side. Randomly placed dots work best.

5. Now that the dots are flowing, add dots to the sides and front of the cabinet body.

6. Paint the eleven robin egg halves with Wicker White. Add dots using Pure Black and the liner brush handle. These dots should be smaller in size than those that are on the cabinet.

7. Using wood glue, attach all the eggs to the door front, and the rooster to the top of the cabinet. Replace the door.

8. Paint the handle with Lipstick Red.

9. Spray the cabinet with matte spray sealer for protection.

Tip

When working with spray sealer, or any spray product, beware of a partially blocked nozzle. This can produce drips and spatters. To clean a nozzle that is a little "gummed up," turn the can upside down and spray until only the aerosol flows, then resume spraying normally. This technique may not work on all cans, but it is worth a try.

Rough Around the Edges

2

There's something that attracts us to surfaces that look like they've survived years of hard use with the scars to prove it. That's one reason the antique business is alive and well. You don't have to shop the antique malls, however, to bring that aged, weathered look into your home.

The projects in this section all have rustic charm and although they may look old, they're not. You will be amazed at what a little sandpaper and antiquing medium can accomplish. No one has to know that box on your mantle isn't a prized family heirloom—yet!

Pony Print CD Holder

Watching old cowboy movies and seeing all the great patterns on the backs of the horses inspired this great CD holder. This strong style statement can be just the thing to spice up any room.

Materials

wooden CD holder
(Jeff McWilliams Designs)

FolkArt Paints:
School Bus Yellow
Warm White

FolkArt Artists' Pigments:
Pure Black

crackle medium

Bucket Brown antiquing medium

metal knob and hinges

$\frac{1}{2}$-inch (12mm) flat brush

$\frac{3}{4}$-inch (19mm) stencil brush

1-inch (25mm) flat brush

clean rag

medium-grade sandpaper

tack cloth

matte spray sealer

1. Sand and prep the surface. Paint the entire interior and exterior of the cabinet with two coats of Warm White, sanding between coats.

2. Using the $\frac{3}{4}$-inch (19mm) stencil brush and Pure Black, pounce the spots of the pony print onto the sides and front of the cabinet. Refer to the photo for placement ideas, and have some of the spots wrap around the sides of the cabinet. Try and think of the spot shapes as clouds, pouncing solid color in the center and less color as you work your way toward the edges. Remember you can make the spots bigger, but it's hard to make them smaller again.

3. Brush two coats of crackle medium onto the roof of the house and onto the trim around the base. Follow the directions on the bottle for specific drying and recoating times.

4. Quickly brush School Bus Yellow over the dried crackle medium using long, smooth strokes. Allow to dry.

5. Use a rag to wipe the entire cabinet with the Bucket Brown antiquing medium. This should age the cabinet and blend the colors of the spots together. Make sure to antique the roof also. Wipe off the excess medium with a clean rag.

6. Spray the cabinet with matte spray sealer for protection. Attach the door to the cabinet with the metal hinges and screw in the metal knob.

Tip

Sometimes working on large projects can cause pain or discomfort in the hand that does the painting. One way to make your brush easier and more comfortable to grip is to place a pencil grip around the handle. The sponge from a foam hair roller works great for larger-handled brushes.

Chili Pepper Cabinet

Add some spice to a dull kitchen with the bold, fiery, southwest flavor of this chili cabinet. Place the cabinet on a counter or on a shelf in the kitchen or dining room.

Materials

wooden cubby (Walnut Hollow)

wooden glue-ons:
2 rectangles, to fit wallpaper cutouts (Provo Craft)

FolkArt Paints:
English Mustard
Lipstick Red
School Bus Yellow
Teddy Bear Tan

FolkArt Artists' Pigments:
Red Light
Yellow Light

chili pepper wallpaper cutouts (or other paper images)

$\frac{1}{2}$-inch (12mm) flat brush

$\frac{1}{2}$-inch (12mm) stencil brush

$\frac{3}{4}$-inch (19mm) stencil brush

1-inch (25mm) flat brush

medium-grade sandpaper

tack cloth

wood glue

matte spray sealer

1. Sand and prep the cabinet. Paint the entire surface of the cabinet inside and out with two coats of Yellow Light, sanding lightly between coats.

2. Using the $\frac{3}{4}$-inch (19mm) stencil brush, pounce School Bus Yellow over the body of the cabinet. The coverage should be light, allowing the undercoat to shine through. When the School Bus Yellow is completely dry, pounce a very light coat of Red Light around the surface. This will create the fiery look of hot peppers.

3. Pounce the top of the cabinet with Lipstick Red, avoiding solid coverage. Pounce Lipstick red on the door knobs also.

4. Paint the rectangles with Teddy Bear Tan. Use the $\frac{1}{2}$-inch (12mm) stencil brush to pounce the edges of the rectangles with English Mustard for a worn effect. This will also allow the rectangles to "pop" off the surface of the doors.

5. Following the directions on the label, add the chili pepper wallpaper cutouts to the rectangle panels. If you are using paper images, apply the paper with découpage medium.

6. Glue the rectangles to the doors with wood glue.

7. Spray the cabinet with matte spray sealer for protection.

Tip

When pouncing with a brush to create texture, the amount of pressure that is applied will greatly affect the color and the detection of a brush pattern. Light pressure usually gives more of a lacy look, while heavy pressure smashes the color together more, and leaves less of a texture.

Bamboo Cabinet

Asian influence is captured in this cabinet. This piece would be useful for storage in a bathroom or bedroom. Although bamboo represents good luck, you could try another stencil to create a completely different look.

Materials

wooden wall cabinet
(Jeff McWilliams Designs)

Apple Barrel Paints:
  Burnt Sienna
  Nutmeg Brown

FolkArt Paints:
  English Mustard
  Olive Green
  Sunflower
  Warm White

FolkArt Artists' Pigments:
  Hauser Light Green
  Hauser Medium Green

crackle medium

metal branch knob

½-inch (12mm) flat brush

½-inch (12mm) stencil brush

1-inch (25mm) flat brush

sea sponge

bamboo stencil

stencil tape

medium-grade sandpaper

tack cloth

wood glue

matte spray sealer

1. Sand and prep the cabinet. Paint the cabinet, inside and out, with two coats of Warm White, sanding between coats.

2. Using the sea sponge, randomly dab the cabinet and the edge of the door with Burnt Sienna. Make sure to allow lots of the Warm White undercoat to show through. Dab on this dark color sparingly, so the cabinet doesn't look too heavy.

3. When the Burnt Sienna is dry, sponge on the Nutmeg, again using loose, random patterns. When this is completely dry, sponge the English Mustard over the other two colors. This will bring a little punch to the color mix. I chose to leave the shelves lighter than the rest of the cabinet for contrast. You could also make the shelves darker to add contrast.

4. Paint the insert section of the door with Sunflower.

5. Brush on two thick coats of crackle medium. Follow the directions on the crackle bottle for drying time and recoating suggestions.

6. Brush Warm White over the crackle medium and wait for it to dry before going on to the next step.

7. Following the instructions on the stencil package, use Hauser Light Green, Hauser Medium Green and Olive Green to stencil and shade the bamboo branch on the cabinet door.

8. Use the ½-inch (12mm) flat brush to trim the top and bottom of the cabinet with Hauser Light Green.

9. Spray the cabinet with matte spray sealer for protection.

Garden Vegetables Bin

Gardening and vegetables evoke simpler times and the warmth of family. Capture these feelings in this rustic textured storage bin. It is a welcome addition to a kitchen counter or a shelf in the great room.

Materials

wooden three-drawer cabinet (Wayne's Woodenware)

wooden glue-ons:
  3 drums (Provo Crafts)
  1 carrot (Provo Craft)
  1 tree (Provo Craft)
  1 tomato (Provo Craft)
  4 angel bodies, large (Bear With Us)

FolkArt Paints:
  Fresh Foliage
  Glazed Carrots
  Hunter Green
  Poppy Red
  Sunflower

FolkArt Artists' Pigments:
  Hauser Medium Green
  Red Light

découpage medium

Bucket Brown antiquing medium

fine-point permanent black marker

paper grocery sack

½-inch (12mm) flat brush

½-inch (12mm) stencil brush

1-inch (25mm) flat brush

2 foam brushes

medium-grade sandpaper

tack cloth

wood glue

matte spray sealer

1. Sand and prep the bin and the drawers. Paint the entire cabinet, including the inside and outside of the drawers, with Hauser Medium Green. Apply two coats, sanding between coats.

2. Cut pieces from a paper grocery sack large enough to completely cover the sides and divider sections in the front of the cabinet, allowing a little extra paper around the edges. Using the foam brush, paint a light coat of découpage medium on one side of the cabinet. (I find it is easier to work one side at a time.) After the side is coated in découpage medium, smooth a piece of paper over the wet medium, then cover the paper with additional medium. After the découpage medium is dry, trim off any excess paper. Repeat the process for the front and remaining side of the cabinet. This gives a leathery, textured finish to your piece.

3. Cover the entire cabinet, including the paper sack sides, with antiquing medium, using a clean foam brush.

4. Paint the three drums with Sunflower, the carrot with Glazed Carrots and the tree with Fresh Foliage. Paint the top of the carrot and the stem area of the tomato with Fresh Foliage. Paint the tomato with Poppy Red.

5. Using the ½-inch (12mm) stencil brush, pounce the top of the tree with Hunter Green. Be careful not to cover all the Fresh Foliage underneath.

6. Cover the vegetables and the drums with antiquing medium. Allow to dry.

7. Use the permanent marker to add the details on the vegetables.

8. Paint the ball top of the angel bodies with Red Light and the body Hauser Medium Green. Paint the trim on the top and bottom of the cabinet with Red Light using the ½-inch (12mm) flat brush.

9. Attach the painted glue-ons with wood glue, using the photo as a guide. Spray the cabinet with the matte spray sealer for protection.

Tip

When using antiquing medium, if too much is applied and the result is muddy, wait for the medium to dry, then go back over it with a bit of fine steel wool to remove areas you'd like to highlight.

Attic Ads Boxes

The warmth and charm of rustic Americana can be found in these decorative boxes. Use them as a grouping in any part of the house.

Materials

wooden boxes: (Walnut Hollow)
Cornice Box
Classic Box
Recipe Box

wooden glue-ons:
3 roosters (Provo Craft)
4 girl toy parts (Lara's Crafts)
4 finial dowel caps (Lara's Crafts)
4 knobs (Lara's Crafts)

FolkArt Paints:
Warm White

FolkArt Artists' Pigments:
Light Red Oxide
Pure Black
Turner's Yellow

découpage medium

antiquing medium

crackle medium

outdated issues of Farmers' Almanac or antique ads

metal hinged clasp

¹/₂-inch (12mm) flat brush

¹/₂-inch (12mm) stencil brush

1-inch (25mm) flat brush

2 foam brushes

chicken wire stencil

craft knife

clean rag

medium-grade sandpaper

tack cloth

wood glue

matte spray sealer

1. Sand and prep the box surfaces. Basecoat the boxes inside and out with two coats of Turner's Yellow, sanding lightly between coats.

2. Disassemble Farmers' Almanac issues. Look for ads, recipes or articles that include old-fashioned images of chickens or farm animals. I used some of the planting calendars for interest. Cut out the desired images. Using a foam brush, lightly brush découpage medium onto the side surfaces of the boxes, keeping the lids closed. Now adhere the cutouts, covering the sides (including recipe box hinges) of each box, overlapping some of the images. Do not cover the tops or bottoms of the boxes. Don't worry if some of the images extend past the sides; just trim them to fit. Also, don't worry about overlapping the gap between the lid and the box; it will be sliced later. When all the cutouts have been placed, brush a coat of découpage medium over the newsprint images. Carefully smooth out the air bubbles along the way. Work on only one side at a time, applying the découpage medium fairly thinly. After the almanac pieces are covered, brush a coat of découpage medium over the entire box to seal the surface in preparation for the antiquing coat. Using a craft knife, separate the top from the bottom of each box. Follow the indentation through the paper, where the lid and the box meet. Sand any rough edges.

3. After the découpage medium is completely dry, apply the antiquing medium using a foam brush to the entire surface of each box. Use a clean rag to remove the excess antiquing medium. You might choose to sand the edges of the box lightly before antiquing it, to age the look even further.

4. Using the ¹/₂-inch (12mm) stencil brush, and Pure Black paint, stencil the chicken wire pattern around the bottom sections of each box.

5. Paint the feet for all three boxes (girl toy parts, finial dowel caps and knobs) with Light Red Oxide. Paint the rooster cutouts with Light Red Oxide as well. Two coats work best for even coverage.

6. Apply two coats of crackle medium to the rooster cutouts. Follow the directions on the bottle for drying time between coats.

7. Paint the roosters with Warm White. Antique all of the feet and the roosters with antiquing medium. Use the rag to remove excess stain while wet.

8. Use wood glue to attach the feet and the roosters to the tops and bottoms of the boxes. I used the knobs for the cornice box, the finial dowel caps for the classic box and the girl toy parts for the recipe box.

9. Spray the boxes with matte spray sealer for durability and protection, and then add the metal clasp to the finished recipe box.

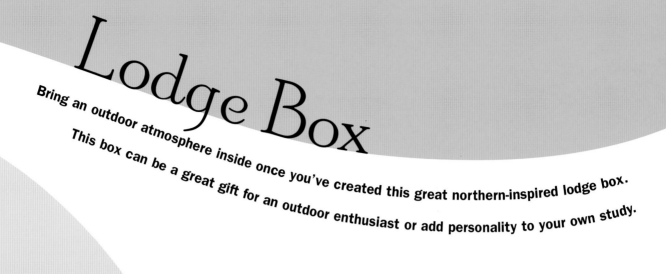

Lodge Box

Bring an outdoor atmosphere inside once you've created this great northern-inspired lodge box. This box can be a great gift for an outdoor enthusiast or add personality to your own study.

Materials

wooden ball foot Lancaster trunk (Walnut Hollow)

wooden glue-ons:
1 drawer knob
1 oar (Lara's Crafts)
1 bear (Lara's Crafts)
1 moon (Lara's Crafts)
1 rectangle (Lara's Crafts)
3 trees (Lara's Crafts)
2 bass fish (Lara's Crafts)
1 fish (Darice)
2 moose (Lara's Crafts)
1 canoe (Lara's Crafts)

Apple Barrel Paints:
Leaf Green

FolkArt Paints:
Aspen Green
Barnyard Red
Coastal Blue
Coffee Bean
Teddy Bear Tan
Thicket

FolkArt Artists' Pigments:
Medium Yellow

pecan stain

foam brush

1/2-inch (12mm) flat brush

1/2-inch (12mm) stencil brush

1-inch (25mm) flat brush

painters' tape

ruler

pencil

medium-grade sandpaper

tack cloth

wood glue

matte spray sealer

1. Sand the box and stain the interior and exterior with the pecan stain and a foam brush.

2. Using a ruler, pencil and painters' tape, and considering the size of each wooden glue-on, mask off rectangles to be used as backgrounds for the various decorative elements. Refer to the photo for placement and color ideas, and leave about $\frac{1}{4}$" (6mm) between each color block. Paint the rectangles with Aspen Green, Medium Yellow, Barnyard Red, Coffee Bean and Teddy Bear Tan. After all of the rectangles have been painted, sand the box lightly to distress the painted areas.

3. Paint the oar and the drawer knob with Barnyard Red.

4. Paint the bear and the rectangle with Coffee Bean.

5. Paint the moon with Medium Yellow.

6. Paint the trees and the feet on the bottom of the box with Leaf Green.

7. Paint one bass fish with Thicket, one bass fish with Coastal Blue and the other fish with Aspen Green.

8. Paint the two moose and the canoe with Teddy Bear Tan.

9. After all the pieces are dry, sand the edges lightly for a distressed look.

10. Referring to the photo for placement, glue the pieces on the box.

11. Spray the box with two coats of matte sealer for protection.

Tip

I usually prepare for a project like this by taping the elements on the surface where I want them to go to get the best feel for placement before beginning my project.

Child's Play

3

At first glance the projects in this section appear to be for children. In reality, that includes all of us, for we all have a child within—if not several of our own. Who among us doesn't secretly want things labeled with our name to spell out exactly who we are? Haven't you ever thought of creating a chest where you can store things that belong only to you?

As you and your children scan the projects in this section, let your imaginations play together—and don't even try to contain your excitement at the thought of creating something magical.

Sunflower Mini Chair

This cute little chair can add a lot of impact to the wall in a child's room. It is just the right size for a favorite doll or stuffed animal.

Materials

wooden flower chair with bird

wooden glue-ons:
*14 micro mini apples
(Lara's Crafts)*

Apple Barrel Paints:
Cobalt Blue

FolkArt Paints:
Blue Ink
Glazed Carrots
Green
Lipstick Red
School Bus Yellow
Tangerine
Warm White

FolkArt Artists' Pigments:
Medium Yellow

$1/2$-inch (12mm) flat brush

$1/2$-inch (12mm) stencil brush

$3/4$-inch (19mm) stencil brush

1-inch (25mm) flat brush

medium-grade sandpaper

tack cloth

wood glue

matte spray sealer

1. Sand and prep the chair and the bird. Basecoat the seat of the chair with Warm White using the 1-inch (25mm) flat brush. Allow to dry. Using the $3/4$-inch (19mm) stencil brush, pounce the seat with Green. Pounce lightly, so that some of the Warm White will show through.

2. Use the 1-inch (25mm) flat brush to paint the legs and the back uprights with Blue Ink, applying two coats for the best coverage.

3. Using the $1/2$-inch (12mm) flat brush and Glazed Carrots, paint the flower on the back of the chair with two coats of paint. Continue the petals onto the uprights. Allow the paint to dry.

4. Pounce School Bus Yellow onto the sunflower, using the $1/2$-inch (12mm) stencil brush, to form the center of the flower. When dry, pounce on a little Medium Yellow in the center to add contrast.

5. Using the $1/2$-inch (12mm) flat brush, brush Tangerine highlights around the perimeters of the petals. Paint the cross pieces around the legs of the chair with Tangerine.

6. Paint the mini apples with Lipstick Red, and let dry. Paint the body of the bird with Cobalt Blue and the bird's beak with Medium Yellow. Paint the stick the bird sits on Medium Yellow as well.

7. When everything is dry, glue the apples around the seat of the chair, spacing them about every $1^{1}/2$" (3.81cm). Glue the stick of the bird into the hole at the top of the chair.

8. Spray the chair with matte spray sealer for protection.

"My Name" Frame

While these frames sport children's names, any title or phrase could be substituted to personalize the frame's contents. By regularly changing the photos inside these name frames, you can keep a record of daily life.

Materials

(SNIPS AND SNAILS)

wooden square frame (Walnut Hollow)

wooden glue-ons:
1 crappie (Bear with Us)
1 blue gill (Bear With Us)
1 catfish (Bear With Us)
wooden alphabet letters
(Jeff McWilliams Designs)

FolkArt Paints:
Fresh Foliage

FolkArt Artists' Pigments:
Cobalt Blue

crackle medium

1/2-inch (12mm) flat brush

1-inch (25mm) flat brush

medium-grade sandpaper

tack cloth

wood glue

matte spray sealer

(SUGAR AND SPICE)

wooden rectangle frame (Walnut Hollow)

wooden glue-ons:
wooden alphabet letters
(Jeff McWilliams Designs)

FolkArt Paints:
Hot Pink
Winter White

crackle medium

1/2-inch (12mm) flat brush

1/2-inch (12mm) stencil brush

1-inch (25mm) flat brush

medium-grade sandpaper

matte spray sealer

tack cloth

wood glue

SNIPS AND SNAILS

1. Sand and prep the frame, then paint the entire surface with two coats of Fresh Foliage, sanding lightly between coats.

2. Brush on two heavy coats of crackle medium. Follow the instructions on the label for drying and recoating.

3. Quickly brush the surface of the frame with Cobalt Blue. To allow the crackling to work well, this should be done with long, smooth strokes.

4. Paint the fish and the letters with two coats of Fresh Foliage.

5. Adhere the fish and letter glue-ons with wood glue, referring to the photo for placement ideas.

6. Spray the frame with matte spray sealer for protection.

SUGAR AND SPICE

1. Sand and prep the frame, then paint the entire surface with two coats of Hot Pink, sanding lightly between coats.

2. Brush on two heavy coats of crackle medium. Follow the instructions on the label for drying and recoating.

3. Quickly brush on a coat of Winter White using long, smooth strokes. This allows the crackling to work well.

4. Paint the letters with two coats of Hot Pink. When dry, pounce the surface of the letters with Winter White using the 1/2-inch (12mm) stencil brush. This will provide some contrast while allowing the letters to blend with the background.

5. Adhere the letter glue-ons with wood glue, referring to the photo for placement ideas.

6. Spray the frame with matte spray sealer for protection.

Tip

This technique can be accomplished with any two colors, or any number of different glue-ons. Select contrasting colors for the greatest impact. You could make several frames in various colors to coordinate with a fabric used in the room.

My Own Toybox

This box can be a great place to put treasured things throughout the years. That special rock or feather can be kept safely out of the way in this personalized storage box.

Materials

wooden toybox

wooden glue-ons:
*2 squares, 2" (51mm)
(Lara's Crafts)
1 circle, 3" (76mm) (Lara's Crafts)
alphabet letters
(Jeff McWilliams Designs)
1 doll head, 2½" (64mm)
(Lara's Crafts)*

FolkArt Paints:
*Green
Lemon Custard
Lipstick Red
Purple
Winter White*

FolkArt Artists' Pigments:
Medium Yellow

½-inch (12mm) flat brush

¾-inch (19mm) stencil brush

1-inch (25mm) flat brush

medium-grade sandpaper

tack cloth

wood glue

matte spray sealer

1. Sand and prep the box. Paint the box inside and out with two coats of Medium Yellow, sanding lightly between coats. Make sure to include the trim on the bottom and the edge of the box top.

2. Using the ¾-inch (19mm) stencil brush, lightly pounce Winter White onto the box top and bottom. Do not pounce on the trim. If you get too much white on the box, go back and pounce more yellow over the top. Allow the box to dry, then pounce Lemon Custard over the white. This will give you three layers of color.

3. Use the ½-inch (12mm) flat brush to paint Green over the yellow trim on the top and bottom of the box, but paint lightly enough to allow some yellow to show through.

4. Paint the squares and the circle with Lipstick Red. After they dry, sand the edges and recoat.

5. Paint the letters and the doll head with Purple. After the paint is completely dry, lightly sand the edges of the letters and the doll head to create a distressed finish.

6. Glue a red square in the centers of each side and the circle in the center of the top, using wood glue. Now adhere the doll head to the top of the box and the letters to the front of the box.

7. Spray the box with matte spray sealer for protection.

Dragonfly Picnic Chest

This bold colored chest has many uses for old and young alike. After it's finished, this picnic-inspired chest will instigate a few giggles along with lunch!

Materials

wooden chest
(Wayne's Woodenware)

Apple Barrel Paints:
  Cobalt Blue
  Hot Pink

FolkArt Paints:
  Cayman Blue
  Green
  Lipstick Red
  Red Violet
  School Bus Yellow
  Winter White

FolkArt Artists' Pigments:
  Medium Yellow
  Pure Black
  Pure Orange
  Yellow Citron

fine-point permanent black marker

no. 1 script liner brush

1-inch (25mm) flat brush

bugs and flowers stencil and stamp kit

medium-grade sandpaper

tack cloth

wood glue

matte spray sealer

1. Sand and prep the chest. Paint the outside with Winter White, using two coats and sanding lightly between coats.

2. Referring to the photo for placement, stamp dragonflies, ladybugs, butterflies and flowers onto the surface of the box and the lid.

COLOR DETAILS:

Dragonfly Body	Yellow Citron
Dragonfly Wings	Cayman Blue
Flower Stem/Leaves	Green
Petals	Red Violet
Flower Center	Hot Pink
Ladybug Body	Lipstick Red
Ladybug Head	Pure Black
Butterfly Wings	School Bus Yellow
Butterfly Body	Pure Orange

3. Paint the body of the box with two coats of Medium Yellow, leaving a $1/4$" (6mm) white area around each of the stamped images.

4. Paint the lid of the box with two coats of Cobalt Blue, leaving a $1/4$" (6mm) white area around each of the stamped images.

5. Paint the feet with Cobalt Blue.

6. Using the no. 1 script liner brush, paint stripes of Winter White across the lid and body of the box. Do not cross the stamped areas.

7. Use the permanent black marker to roughly outline the stamped images, and to create random dashed lines showing movement of the bugs. See the photo for ideas.

8. Seal the box with matte spray sealer.

Princess Chair

With its bold colors and striking presence, this fantastic throne can be a great showpiece in any child's room. The wooden glue-ons used in this particular project follow a floral theme, but you could draw from other decorative elements in the room to suit the royal fancy of your own prince or princess.

Materials

wooden princess chair
(Jeff McWilliams Designs)

wooden glue-ons:
  5 flowers (Provo Craft)
  3 caps (Lara's Crafts)
  2 plates (Lara's Crafts)
  5 circles (Provo Craft)
  5 funky swirls (Provo Craft)
  22 footballs (Lara's Crafts)

Apple Barrel Paints:
  Lavender

FolkArt Paints:
  Bright Green
  Dark Hydrangea
  Green
  Hydrangea
  Magenta
  Red Violet
  Tangerine
  Wicker White

FolkArt Artists' Pigments:
  Butler Magenta
  Medium Yellow

$1/2$-inch (12mm) flat brush
$1/2$-inch (12mm) stencil brush
1-inch (25mm) flat brush
sea sponge
1" (25mm) painters' tape
medium-grade sandpaper
tack cloth
wood glue
matte spray sealer

1. Sand and prep all of the chair components, then paint everything with two coats of Wicker White, sanding lightly between coats.

2. Paint the chair seat and the circular inserts for the tops of the "spires" with a solid coat of Dark Hydrangea. Brush the arms lightly with Dark Hydrangea, allowing the white undercoat to show through.

3. Use painters' tape to mask off stripes on the seat (see step 2 of the Tiny Bubbles Mirror, page 19). Starting at the left side, place the tape vertically across the seat from front to back. Remove every other piece of tape, exposing the Dark Hydrangea.

4. Using the $1/2$-inch (12mm) stencil brush, pounce the open areas lightly with Wicker White. Make sure you don't create a solid line.

5. Using a damp sea sponge, dab Hydrangea randomly over the entire surface of the chair, including the backside, creating no noticeable pattern.

6. Paint the edges of the back and front of the chair Dark Hydrangea for contrast.

7. Paint the flower pieces with Dark Hydrangea. Paint the caps and the plates with Wicker White.

8. Paint two circles the Red Violet, two with Tangerine and one with Magenta. These will make up the bottom sections of the swirl flowers.

9. Paint two swirls with Medium Yellow, two with Lavender and one with Butler Magenta for the tops of the swirl flowers.

10. Paint nine footballs with Green and thirteen footballs with Bright Green for the leaves of the swirl flowers.

11. Referring to the photo for placement, use wood glue to attach all the glue-ons to the chair. Once these have dried, use the glue and screws provided to assemble the chair.

12. Spray the chair with matte spray sealer for protection.

Slightly Sophisticated

Are there one or two spots in your home that could use a touch of style and sophistication? Any of the projects in this section would suit your needs wonderfully.

Being stylish doesn't have to mean being trendy. Whether you desire something classic, like the Textured Candle Holders, or something with pizzazz like the Martini Tote, you won't have to spend a fortune to add charm to your room with these great accessories. Each one would also serve as a lovely gift for that discerning friend.

Gentleman's Club Box

There are few projects designed for the men in this world. Here is a great masculine storage box to make for a friend or yourself. Its bold red leather-like finish can add warmth to any desktop or dresser.

Materials

purse box (Walnut Hollow)

FolkArt Paints:
Lipstick Red

FolkArt Artists' Pigments:
Pure Black

FolkArt Mediums:
Folk Art Thickener or Extender

cherry stain

4 metal knobs

1 metal cabinet handle

$1/2$-inch (12mm) flat brush

1-inch (25mm) flat brush

foam brush

texturing tool or sea sponge

disposable plastic plate

drill with $1/8$" (3mm) bit

clean rag

medium sand paper

tack cloth

matte spray sealer

1. Sand the box surface. Stain the inside of the box with cherry stain, using a foam brush. Wipe away any excess stain with a clean rag. Paint the entire outside surface of the box with two coats of Lipstick Red, sanding lightly between coats.

2. Using the disposable plate as a mixing bowl, mix equal parts of Folk Art Thickener and Pure Black paint. This will create a glaze for the texturing process. Dampen the texturing tool (found in the faux finishing section of the paint department) or sea sponge with water before pouncing it into the glaze. Practice on scrap paper before pouncing onto the box. It is critical to not have too much paint on the tool, so blot off any excess before moving to the box surface. Pounce the glaze mixture onto the box, starting with the back and moving around the box to include the top, front, sides and bottom. Keep the color heavier on the edges and lighter toward the middle, remembering that it's easier to add more color than to remove it. After the box is covered, wait five minutes and then proceed to add more glaze with the tool where necessary. This step will give the box a nice layered look.

3. When the box is completely dry, spray the surface with matte spray sealer for protection.

4. Allow the sealer to dry completely. Using the drill and the $1/8$" (3mm) bit, make four holes in the bottom of the box for the four knobs that will serve as feet, and two holes in the appropriate part of the lid for the handle. Add this hardware to finish.

Tip

When using several different paints and mediums in a project, it is best to stick to one brand. Problems such as peeling or bubbling can sometimes occur when mixing brands. After having tried the products of several different manufacturers, and becoming more aware of their properties, you can feel better about risking their compatibility.

Bed & Birdseed House

The roof of this house has such personality. Although your local feathered friends would love this retreat, this is too special to put outside! A gardening friend would love this as a gift as well.

Materials

large wooden birdhouse
(Walnut Hollow)

wooden glue-ons:
    4 drapery finials
    1 finial dowel cap (Lara's Crafts)

FolkArt Paints:
    School Bus Yellow
    Thunder Blue
    Warm White

crackle medium

antiquing medium

$^1/_2$-inch (12mm) flat brush

$^1/_2$-inch (12mm) stencil brush

1-inch (25mm) flat brush

1" (25mm) painters' tape

foam brush

ruler

pencil

clean rag

medium-grade sandpaper

tack cloth

wood glue

matte spray sealer

1. Sand and prep the birdhouse, then paint the entire surface with Warm White. Use two coats of paint, sanding lightly between coats.

2. Brush two coats of crackle medium onto the body of the house. Follow the directions on the bottle for specific drying details.

3. Quickly brush a coat of Thunder Blue paint onto the body of the birdhouse.

4. On one side of the roof, locate the exact center top to bottom and side to side; mark this spot with a pencil. Draw a light horizontal line at this mark across the roof. Beginning at the center mark and moving out along this line toward both edges, make a mark every 1$^1/_2$" (38mm). Next, locate and mark the centers of the top and bottom edges of the roof; then beginning again at the center point, measure and mark every 1$^1/_2$" (38mm) along each edge. Now measure the distance between the center line and the top edge. At half this distance, draw a light horizontal line. Draw another line at half the distance from the center line to the bottom edge.

    You now have three equally spaced lines. Find the center of the top line and mark $^3/_4$" (19mm) to the left and right of this point, then make marks every 1$^1/_2$" (38mm) from those points to the edges. Repeat for the bottom line.

    Now connect the dots diagonally and rule these lines lightly. There should be a visible pattern of diamonds. Use painters' tape to mask off and paint one diamond at a time, using School Bus Yellow and the $^1/_2$-inch (12mm) stencil brush. Be sure to allow the paint to dry before repositioning the tape. Repeat this process for the other side of the roof.

5. Paint the drapery finials with Thunder Blue and School Bus Yellow, referring to the photo for specific color placement.

6. Paint the finial dowel cap School Bus Yellow. This will become the perch on your birdhouse. Attach with wood glue, below the entry hole.

7. Paint the bottom edge of the birdhouse with School Bus Yellow.

8. After all the paint is completely dry, antique the entire house, including the four drapery finial feet and the finial dowel cap, using the foam brush. Wipe off excess antiquing medium with a clean rag.

9. Spray the entire surface of the birdhouse with matte spray sealer.

Silver Leaf Game Box

Losing a game of checkers isn't all that bad with this up-scale game board. Doubling as a storage chest for the pieces, this box is created with a metallic finish to be used in any room in the house.

Materials

round stacking box

wooden glue-ons:
23 birch RH plugs, ⅜" (10mm)
(Lara's Crafts)
16 birch RH plugs, 1" (25mm)
(Lara's Crafts)
4 doll heads, 2½" (64mm)
(Lara's Crafts)

FolkArt Metallic Paints:
Blue Sapphire

FolkArt Artists' Pigments:
Pure Black

½-inch (12mm) flat brush

¾-inch (19mm) stencil brush

1-inch (25mm) flat brush

foil adhesive

silver leaf

1" (25mm) painters' tape

ruler

pencil

clean rag

medium-grade sandpaper

tack cloth

wood glue

high-gloss spray sealer

1. Sand and prep the box surface. Paint the inside and outside with two coats of Pure Black, sanding lightly between coats. Also paint the ⅜" (10mm) wooden plugs with Pure Black.

2. When dry, glue the black plugs to the perimeter of the box lid, evenly spacing from top to bottom and from side to side.

3. Coat a small section of the box with foil adhesive. Following the directions on the silver leaf package, apply the leaf. Repeat, working with small sections at a time, until the entire box is covered. Use the ¾-inch (19mm) stencil brush to work the silver leaf into the nooks and crannies of the box lid, and around the plugs.

4. Use the Pure Black paint as an antiquing medium over the silver leaf to knock the shiny finish off the surface. Use a clean rag to apply the paint to the surface and to wipe off the excess.

5. Use the ruler and the pencil to mark off a game board in the center of the box lid. Use the painters' tape to mask off 1" (25mm) checks on the game board. Once the tape is in place, pounce Blue Sapphire onto the game board to create the checks.

6. Paint eight of the larger plugs with Blue Sapphire and the other eight with Pure Black. These will be the playing pieces. Also paint the doll heads with Blue Sapphire for the four feet of the box.

7. Glue the feet onto the game board using wood glue. Spray both the box and the game pieces with a coat of high-gloss sealer.

Tip

When using metallic leafing, you can save the small bits and pieces that collect when you brush the excess off. These small pieces can be used for future projects to fill in cracks and crevices, or you can use them as embellishments in other creative endeavors, such as papercrafts.

Martini Tote

This funky metallic piece does not have to be left at the bar. It can have multiple uses in your home, or you can give it to the friend that has everything. Use it to hold bar supplies, or in the kitchen for sheer impact.

Materials

wooden tote, small
(Wayne's Woodenware)

wooden glue-ons:
  10 robin eggs (Lara's Crafts)
  4 girl toy parts (Lara's Crafts)

Apple Barrel Paints:
  Bright Red

FolkArt Artists' Pigments:
  Hauser Light Green
  Pure Black

FolkArt Metallic Paints:
  Peridot
  Sequin Black
  Silver Sterling

$\frac{1}{2}$-inch (12mm) flat brush

$\frac{1}{2}$-inch (12mm) stencil brush

1-inch (25mm) flat brush

1" (25mm) painters' tape

ruler

pencil

medium-grade sandpaper

tack cloth

wood glue

high-gloss spray sealer

---

1. Sand and prep the tote. Paint the entire surface, inside and out with Pure Black, applying two coats and sanding lightly between coats.

2. Brush Hauser Light Green onto the inside of the tote, but do not cover the black undercoat completely.

3. On the tall sides of the tote, run a strip of painters' tape horizontally between the two open ends of the opposite sides so that you have a continuous square shape on the lower half of the box. The upper portions of the tall sides will remain black.

On the front side of the box, use the ruler to locate the exact center from top to bottom and from side to side. Mark this spot with a pencil. Draw a light horizontal line through this center point, continuing all around the box. Make a dot every 1½" (38mm) along this line. Make marks at these same intervals along the top and bottom edges. Now measure half the distance between the center line and the top edge, and draw another light horizontal line, continuing around the box. Draw another line halfway between the center line and bottom edge.

You now have three equally spaced lines. Find the center of the top line on the front of the box, then mark ³⁄₄" (19mm) to the left and right of this point. Measure and mark every 1½" (38mm) from those points all around the box. Repeat for the bottom line.

Now connect the dots diagonally and rule these lines lightly. There should be a visible pattern of diamonds all around the tote. Use painters' tape to mask off the pattern, then paint one diamond at a time, using Silver Sterling and the ½-inch (12mm) stencil brush. After you paint one diamond, allow it to dry, then remove the tape and repeat the process with another diamond until every other diamond is painted silver.

4. Paint the handle of the tote with Silver Sterling.

5. Paint the girl toy parts and the robin eggs with two coats of Peridot.

6. Paint the balls on the ends of the girl toy parts with Bright Red. Use Bright Red to paint pimentos on the ends of the robin eggs.

7. Randomly glue the olives onto the diamond-painted section of the tote. Glue the girl toy parts to the bottom of the tote for feet.

8. Spray the tote with high-gloss sealer for protection.

Textured Candle Holders

The dramatic effect of candles on a mood may be enhanced even further by these candlesticks. Their versatile design will fit anywhere, from a formal setting to a soapy bath retreat.

Materials

3 wooden handrail spindles
(use various styles)

1 ball cap

wooden glue-ons:
  1 candle cup (Lara's Crafts)
  12 doll heads, 1" (25mm)
  (Lara's Crafts)
  8 doll heads, 1¼" (32mm)
  (Lara's Crafts)
  3 round circles, 2¼" (57mm)
  (Lara's Crafts)
  1 cube, 2" (51mm) (Lara's Crafts)
  1 powder box lid (Lara's Crafts)
  4 blocks, 2¾" × 2¾" × ¾"
  (70mm × 70mm × 19mm)
  1 block, 3½" × 3½" × ¾"
  (89mm × 89mm × 19mm)

FolkArt Metallic Paints:
  Antique Copper
  Pure Gold

FolkArt Artists' Pigments:
  Pure Black
  Pure Magenta
  True Burgundy
  Yellow Ochre

½-inch (12mm) flat brush

¾-inch (19mm) stencil brush

1-inch (25mm) flat brush

hand saw

medium-grade sandpaper

tack cloth

wood glue

high-gloss spray sealer

1. Using a hand saw, cut the railing into pieces of five various heights. Vary where the cuts are made to create interest. Sand smooth, then use wood glue to assemble parts to create the candlesticks. Refer to the photo for ideas. When the glue is completely dry, paint the entire surface of each candle holder with two coats of Pure Magenta, sanding lightly between coats.

2. Using the ¾-inch (19mm) stencil brush, pounce True Burgundy over the Pure Magenta on each of the candle holders, to create areas that appear marbled. Take care not to cover all of the Pure Magenta undercoat. While the paint is still wet, pounce Yellow Ochre over the first two colors, allowing the colors to blend, to create some lighter areas and some darker areas.

3. Trim the candle holders using Antique Copper and Pure Gold. Refer to the photo for specific color placement on each candlestick, but remember that your candle holders may not be configured the same way as mine, depending on the spindle styles you chose. Vary your trim colors accordingly.

4. Spray the candle holders with two coats of high-gloss spray sealer.

Tip

When working on a project that combines one or more colors to form a texture, if one of the colors ends up looking too distinct, wait for the paint to dry, then reapply a blend of the original basecoat and the dominant color.

Most of the materials used in this book can be found at either an art and craft store or a hardware store. However, if you cannot locate an item listed in the material lists, check with these manufacturers for retail distributors in your area.

RESOURCES

AMERICAN TRADITIONAL STENCILS
442 First New Hampshire Turnpike
Northwood, NH 03261
www.americantraditional.com
(800) 448-6656
(stencils)

BEAR WITH US INC.
3007 S. Kendall Avenue
Independence, MO 64055
BEARWUS@aol.com
(816) 373-3231
(wooden glue-ons, birdhouse)

DARICE INC.
13000 Darice Parkway, Park 82
Strongsville, OH 44149
(800) 321-1494
www.darice.com
(wooden glue-ons)

DELTA TECHNICAL COATINGS
2550 Pellissier Place
Whittier, CA 90601
(800) 423-4135
www.deltacrafts.com
(foil adhesive)

JEFF MCWILLIAMS DESIGNS
702 Holcomb Bridge Road
Norcross, GA 30071
www.jmdonline.net
(cabinet, alphabet letters, chair)

LARA'S CRAFTS
4220 Clay Avenue
Fort Worth, TX 76117
www.larascrafts.com
(800) 232-5272
(wooden glue-ons)

MONA LISA PRODUCTS
Houston Art, Inc
10770 Moss Ridge Road
Houston, TX 77043-1175
(800) 272-3804
www.houstonart.com
(silver leaf)

PLAID ENTERPRISES INC.
Norcross, GA 30091-7600
www.plaidonline.com
(800) 842-4197
(acrylic paints, mediums, brushes)

PROVO CRAFT
151 East 3450 North
Spanish Fork, UT 84660
www.provocraft.com
(800) 937-7686
(wooden glue-ons, cabinet)

WALLIES
The McCall Pattern Co.
P. O. Box 3100
Manhattan, KS 66505-3100
(800) 225-2762 ext. 485
www.wallies.com
(wallpaper cutouts)

WALNUT HOLLOW FARMS INC.
1409 State Road 23
Dodgeville, WI 53533
(800) 950-5101
www.walnuthollow.com
(clock base, boxes, frames, trunk, cubby, birdhouse)

WAYNE'S WOODENWARE, INC.
102C S. Fieldcrest Drive
Neenah, WI 54956
(800) 840-1497
www.wayneswoodenware.com
(lamp base, cabinet, tote, chest)

INDEX

The best in creative instruction and inspiration is from North Light Books!

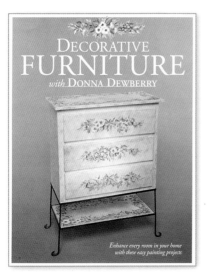

Donna Dewberry shows you how to master her legendary one-stroke technique for painting realistic flowers, fruits and other decorative motifs. Simple step-by-step instructions accompany each project. Guidelines for matching color combinations to existing room schemes enable you to customize every project to fit your décor!

ISBN 1-58180-016-9, paperback, 128 pages, #31662-K

Create classic holiday decorations that everyone will love! You'll find 13 simple painting projects inside, from Santa figures and Christmas card holders to tree ornaments and candy dishes. Each one includes easy-to-follow instructions, step-by-step photographs and simple designs that you can use on candles, fabric, glass and more.

ISBN 1-58180-237-4, paperback, 112 pages, #32012-K

Create thoughtful gifts for special friends and relatives with these easy brush lettering and decorative painting strokes. Jan Belliveau takes you step-by-step through 10 lovely projects, each featuring an uplifting saying. You'll learn the basics of brush lettering and how to develop your own unique style while adding flourishes and flowers to each exquisite gift you create.

ISBN 1-58180-464-4, paperback, 48 pages, #32721-K

Enjoy your spookiest Halloween ever with the help of Margaret Wilson and Robyn Thomas. You'll find 20 simple projects for classic party decorations and home décor. Complete step-by-step photos will guide you in crafting ghoulish Halloween motifs such as pumpkins, ghosts, candy corn and witches on a variety of surfaces.

ISBN 1-58180-382-6, paperback, 80 pages, #32413-K

These books and other fine North Light titles are available from your local art & craft retailer, bookstore, online supplier or by calling 1-800-448-0915.